ACKNOWLEDGMENT!

*The #1 Secret To Command Respect From Your Customers
And How To Spot An Asshole From A Good One*

MARCELLO

Copyright © 2020
Marcello
ACKNOWLEDGMENT!
The #1 Secret To Command Respect From Your Customers
And How To Spot An Asshole From A Good One
All rights reserved.

No part of this publication may be reproduced, distributed, or transmitted in any form or by any means, including photocopying, recording, or other electronic or mechanical methods, without the prior written permission of the publisher, except in the case of brief quotations embodied in critical reviews and certain other non-commercial uses permitted by copyright law.

Marcello

Printed in the United States of America
First Printing 2020
First Edition 2020

ISBN: 979-8671378108

10 9 8 7 6 5 4 3 2 1

ACKNOWLEDGMENT!

TABLE OF CONTENTS

CHAPTER 1..1

Introduction

CHAPTER 2..9

The Subtle Belittling Remarks – The One Above You

CHAPTER 3..15

The Price Denier

CHAPTER 4..19

The Worst Type – The Discount Asker

CHAPTER 5..23

The Dontgiveashit

CHAPTER 6..27

Other Stories

CHAPTER 7..29

Conclusion

CHAPTER 1

INTRODUCTION

The #1 secret and the most important in understanding and profiling your customers for a successful business relationship and for mutual respect is:

ACKNOWLEDGMENT.

Make no mistake though; this isn't a guide on how to be diplomatic with your customers, how to schmooze them or how to conquer them, if you picked up this book because of these reasons, drop me now!

There are plenty of books out there on how to get success and how to succeed in public relations and in business. This is about handling and dealing with all types of customers that will come your way without kissing their boots, without letting them step over you and your dignity. It is about gaining their respect while winning a sale over the phone or face to face or via a quote, and establish a long and healthy business relationship with them. It is about spotting the asshole customer that will just waste a tremendous amount of your time and money.

Just like in a movie, I have only the first 2-3 minutes to grab your attention before I lose you.

Do you have a business? A small or big business? Do you work for yourself? Are you your own boss? It does not matter if you are selling pens, dishwashers, tea, or if you offer a local or national service, if you want to know how to spot the nightmare customer at first glance, keep reading. I will reveal what acknowledgment can do for you, how to use it and how you can take back control of your own business by taking control of your customers and enjoying being your own boss whether you are just starting or not.

Customers are people just like you. For you to understand how to treat a customer, you would want to first examine and understand how you want another business to treat you when buying their service or product.

One day, I had it out with a customer because he would refuse or ignore my several requests to reply to one of my emails. In this email, I put in particularly important information about the warranty of my service and what to expect going forward.

I needed him to ACKNOWLEDGE IT with a simple reply, an "ok" would do, I said. However, over time, this customer kept texting or calling me and every time for help and questions, always about what he needed but

ACKNOWLEDGMENT!

never acknowledging my emails even after asking him to do that several times and after explaining the reason it was so important.

After one week of this nonsensical ping-pong, I confronted him, and I said: Why are you ignoring me when I ask you to reply to that important email of mine? I know you opened it, I know you read it (thanks to email tracking/receipt), but you are not answering it. What's wrong? He says: Oh, I am too busy, I had to take care of this and that, and blah blah blah. I had to tell him there is no excuse, we are all very busy, people work three jobs, and they can still find a second to reply to an email or send a text. That is just unacceptable, I said.

Now, I had already made up my mind and was ready to fire him but wanted to truly see his color and so I asked him why. Why are you ignoring me when I provided you with excellent service? You are seeking more help, which I will be glad to offer, but why can't you respect my service? Note that I said "service" because I am not taking it personally. This isn't a personal matter, but it is still my business, my time, and I won't let someone ignore my requests while they continue to seek my help and for free.

And for whoever thinks this is not a big deal, IT IS! From these details, you know who you're really dealing with. I wanted him to say it and I asked the HOT question: would you do this to one of your customers? Would you ignore them even after several attempts at reaching you? SILENCE! This is when you know you have a chance at getting through his brain. I asked him again, and after a long pause, he finally says: "But you are not my customer. I am paying you!" Wow, I thought. That is how he perceives me or any other individual or companies that offer him a service or product. I see, I said, you think you can treat people like shit just because you are paying them. It does not matter they are earning that money and that they are people, human beings? You pay people to slap them?

I don't think so, bitch! I did not actually curse, there is no need to curse, although it always depends on who you are dealing with. My last words were: I cannot help you further then, find someone else and goodbye. The call ended that way.

Some of you might think you made a mistake, and you lost a customer. Actually, I lost a cancer because this is the typical customer you want to avoid, and this is the attitude you do not want from anyone, which is at the core of this guide.

I met many people like this man, and when I was inexperienced, I put up with some of it, then I learned and came to my conclusions. Here is what this type of

ACKNOWLEDGMENT!

customer will do to you: they will always try to keep a tension or a sense of dissatisfaction towards your service or product as to keep you at bay and under their control. Think of it like a rope, they pull it to keep it tense in the hope you will jump for them at the snap of their fingers, and they will slap your face when you don't jump quick enough. Maybe they do this for a power trip or because they are always trying to get something for free, or because they are simply sick or just do not respect others. Whichever is the reason, this is the customer that will never, never, never ACKNOWLEDGE your service and respect your business.

The word acknowledgment will be typed so often throughout this guide because you will see through some of my stories and experiences, how, they all round up to this very one thing, **they do not acknowledge your services.** Understanding who to avoid will make your business successful, you will only and mainly get positive reviews, gratification, a solid business relationship with those good, repeating customers and a long one; you will go through your day of work with a great sense of direction; you will know what to accomplish; **you will enjoy being your own boss and you will be in control of your own business**.

Now, if you hate what you do in the first place, then change the damn business, follow your goals and dreams, and get yourself a Wayne Dyer book too. Don't be a "yes man," "yes sir," "yes, no problem," you will ruin your business or run it like it's rotten. Do not be a prima donna either, but just respect and treat your customers as you would want them to treat you. It all stems from: don't do to others what you wouldn't want them to do to you. Business is not that different from life if you look at it this way.

Unfortunately, greed gets in the way, and there are plenty of businesses out there in our world that are destroying people and our planet for money. If you are one of them, this book isn't for you, fuck off! It just does not apply to people that do not understand respect. You might be like a mercenary and if so, you already know your bottom line. You wouldn't understand, you couldn't understand, you shouldn't understand.

If you are a good person legitimately trying to build a successful business through honesty and transparency, then this guide is for you. I will help you understand who is in front of you, and hopefully, when you are done reading this whole shebang, you can run your business like a boss and control your customers for better business. Note: I am not trying to have you control a customer in the sense you will be able to manipulate him/her in your

ACKNOWLEDGMENT!

favor, but in the sense you will command respect because you respect them in the first place, and you wish that to be reciprocal.

I also know that in this world, here and there you must compromise, you can't get your way or the right way all the times, but at the very least, you can be better, feel better and always know deep down, you can say NO or FIRE someone you do not want to deal with. Yes, there is an actual thing as firing your customers if you did not know. It is not absurd; it is necessary sometimes.

You might say: Yeah, right! How the hell do I put food on my table if I discard 50% of asshole customers I have?

First, I want to clarify one thing right away: I don't give a shit about what you think if what you think is negative, ignorant and not constructive.

Here is one answer, though: I have done it. I fired many customers, I improved my business and I grew it more successful. I support myself and my family. I am no superior being; you can do it too and so can everyone else. Find an opportunity, work multiple jobs, work your business in the day and uber at night. I see and know people that do it, and they put food on the table.

On the other hand, if you are working for someone and you are not your own boss yet, then think of something, and start your own journey. I cannot offer you courage and guts, you will have to find that on your own, find your own strength.

Bless straightforwardness! People should appreciate when you do not beat around the bush, and you get straight to the point. That person talking to you in a direct, honest and transparent way should be admired and appreciated.

However, some people do not like it when you say things upfront. They'd rather you doublespeak.

The customers that do not like your straightforwardness are to be distanced.

Nothing wrong if you wish to sugar coat something if you do get to the point, though, and tell it how it is in the end. Now there are so many other criteria to factor in before you fire a customer, but you get the point or you will.

CHAPTER 2
THE SUBTLE BELITTLING REMARKS – THE ONE ABOVE YOU

A customer calls you and they ask for your pricing about your service or product. You tell them it costs $100, for example. They say: What??? $100???

STOP! You, the reader, stop here. When you get this from someone, you must ask them immediately: what's with the surprised reaction? And wait to see what they say. That is very important to know why they are surprised. It could be they never called or used the type of business before, and they are not aware of the pricing; maybe it is out of their budget, and they cannot afford it, and nothing is wrong with neither of the above.

It could also be that they do not value your business service or product at $100. That is where you need to pay very much attention. The person that cannot afford it, that is understandable, not everyone has money. The one that does not value your business, and thinks they should pay half of what you bill, **that is the customer you need to avoid.**

Before you distance that customer from your business, though, you wish to find out the intention behind their reaction; ask them simply: why are you surprised? They might say: that is a lot of money.

That needs to be a trigger for the COMPARISON QUESTION.

Ask them: Compared to who? (if it is a service) or to what? (if it's a product)?

This last question will make you understand if they think and/or know your pricing is higher than your competition, in which case, you will discover who's selling for less. You will find out usually (90% of times), that they do not know and when asking them the comparison question, you will get no answer! They usually go in silence mode or deviate from it.

And that is when you know that they think your pricing to be too much as a conjecture in their mind. Maybe you are a plumber, for example, and I know in my area, plumbers work for at around $90/hour on average. If I call a plumber and hear this pricing, I would not get surprised. If I did not know what every other plumber charges per hour, I would solely base it on my view of what a plumber's work should be valued at.

If I do not think much of a plumber's work, then I will probably expect to pay him $20/hour compared to the standard average of my location. If I value his work higher, then I would not get surprised when he says $90/h.

Now this rests on society and the hierarchy created by all of us, by the big corporations, the economy, and who knows what else. We see lawyers as expensive, and if we call a lawyer and he would say: we bill $150/hour or $300/hour, we would be disappointed but not surprised.

And this is valid for every other profession, we know dentists are expensive, and even more expensive, surgeons and operations, medical bills, etc. We each create expectations of what someone's work is to be valued at.

Then there is the type of person that gets surprised not because they are comparing your service/product to someone else of the same profession/field but to themselves. Let's say you are a plumber, and the customer calling you is an electrician. Now you say you charge $90/hour, but the customer as an electrician has always charged his own customers $40 an hour.

He does not value the plumber's work to be better/higher than his electrical work, and as such, the first thought that fires in his mind is:

Who does this motherf…plumber think he is? Why is he charging double than me? It ain't right, it ain't fair, it ain't fit, it ain't proper and it ain't friendly (from Poldark), I shall add, he ain't better than me.

This, sadly, is what goes on in his mind. You will not sell to this guy, I can assure you he will not buy your service or if he does, he will have many reservations. He might also buy your service or product but get sarcastic or will make remarks here and there to send you the message you are expensive.

You thank them for buying from you, and they say something like, you should thank me all right! - after I spent a fortune! And many other little remarks like that along those lines. They will just never appreciate or value your work even if they had to use it due to an emergency, for example, or because they just did not want to bother much doing comparison shopping.

He will never acknowledge your service, never be satisfied, and never fully accept anything else you tell them. **No acknowledgment, no good!**

Whichever the case, ask the comparison question, and talking with them should make you understand if he/she is the customer that does not appreciate or value your service or else.

You can see how everything turns around acknowledgment, and even when it doesn't, you can use the acknowledgment test to discover how good a customer is or how much of an asshole he/she is.

One time, this customer says to me: Wow! You charge

ACKNOWLEDGMENT!

$150/hour, I should have changed business, it takes me days to make that kind of money. And when I hear that, I always reply, you should have!

This is the United States, the land of opportunity where dreams can come true if you are persistent enough, if you believe it hard enough and if you work hard enough. **I spent 23 years of my life learning what I do, and NO ONE shall ever belittle me or you for earning your money.**

If you worked hard enough to get where you are, and you think your work is to be valued at $150/hour, go for it! There are no laws that regulate how much you can charge your customers (for most businesses unless social ones that need regulation); people are free to shop around. You got enough talent, skills and experience, go for it! Are you a master carpenter? A professional? Go for it.

Obviously, you always want to keep an eye on your competition, if everyone else with the same years of experience and talent charges on average $100/hour and you are billing people $400/hour unless justified, you might lose customers. There is no limit to what you can charge and value your service, but make sure you check your competition and/or distinguish yourself to justify the higher pricing.

MARCELLO

CHAPTER 3
THE PRICE DENIER

How much is it again? How much do you charge? How much again? I wish this would be the only call I got throughout the years or one of a few, but that is not the case.

This type of customer actually exists, and no matter how many times you tell them how much you charge, they will not ACKNOWLEDGE your pricing. It is not about being deaf or hard of hearing; they just mentally won't accept your rates.

Real phone conversation:

Customer: How much do you charge?

Me: I charge $95/hour to perform the job.

Customer: Ok, you charge $95/hour, I see. When can you come?

Me: Would tomorrow between 10 am and 11 am work for you?

Customer: Yes, tomorrow is good, and you will come to the house and do it here?

Me: Yes, at completion, you can pay via credit card or cash or via PayPal.

Customer: How much do you charge again?

Me: $95/h

Customer: How much??? (like with an almost surprised tone here)

Me: Ninety-five-dollars-an-hour

Customer: So, you charge $95 to do the job then.

Me: No, Sir, I do not charge a flat fee, it is on a per-hour-basis. Once again, <u>I charge $95 per hour.</u>

Customer: Will you also help me doing…...? (changing the subject now)

Me: Yes, I will do this and that… (Here I go on explaining in more details what tasks I will be performing as to answer his questions)

Customer: Ok, I understand, that is good. So, you are coming tomorrow, and your rates are $95 for the job. Will see you tomorrow then, thanks. (just tried to re-affirm what he thinks he should pay me)

Me: Hold on…hold on! I bill on an hourly basis; this is no flat fee, sir, it is $95 an hour, meaning if I spend 2 hours, it will cost you $190, 3 hours $285, and so on. Is that clear to you how my pricing works? I do not wish to have

ACKNOWLEDGMENT!

misunderstandings. (Now I have to start talking to him like if he is an idiot, I do not mean to, but nonetheless, I will sound that way, we are back to elementary school and basic math.)

Customer: Ah? What? $95 an hour? Uhm…I gotta think about this.

LOL. This is how it ends or other times, it ends that I do not help them because they just will not acknowledge the pricing.

You son of a bitch, stop the pretense and stop bringing me into your I-am-dumb ride. You are most likely smarter than me, don't play the fool and waste my time, yeah?

This is no hard-of-hearing situation, I can assure you and this type of call, I got it so many times over the years I should have a hard time believing this type of attitude even exists, but it does. Obviously, I missed other details, I take their address, name, etc., and a call like this can take easily 15 minutes out of your time and leads to nothing or a bad experience.

Acknowledgment is so important because you know they know, and you know they know that you know. You know they are on the same page as you are, you know there will be no misunderstandings, you know there will be no false expectations because you are setting the right expectations.

MARCELLO

CHAPTER 4
THE WORST TYPE – THE DISCOUNT ASKER

Can you do better? You hear that from the customer that wants to pay less. Now, like before, there could be a few different reasons for asking for a discount.

Here is how I discover the arrogant asshole that just thinks nothing of your service and/or wants to take advantage of you. Meanwhile, they need your skills, and it is not something they could remotely do themselves either. To each, its talent. I know that clearly, this type of person does not or doesn't want to understand that.

You tell them your pricing, evaluation or whatever else, and they say: Can you do better?

That is when I ask: Why? Why do you ask for a discount? Is it because you think my service doesn't deserve it or I won't earn it? Or is it because you do not have much of a budget for it? (Diplomatic way to say you cannot afford it and there is nothing wrong with not being able to afford something or a service.)

They usually all reply the same: well…that is a lot of money! Here is when I tell them that a lot of money is always relative to what you are buying. You can spend half of a million dollars for a big house; half of a million dollars is a lot of money, and that is also getting you a big and beautiful property. You get my point; it is always relative to what you are buying.

And then I finish by saying that is what my competitors bill for this type of work (which is the truth and I study my competition's pricing monthly). Actually, a few professionals will bill you about 20% higher than me. So, if you are asking me for a discount, I can't do that because **I am right-on-the-money already!**

Whether that is true or not, that will be up to you, and there isn't really a true way to find out effectively who's charging in your profession. Always following the example of a plumber, you will find the professional that charges $80/h and the handyman that knows plumbing and does that on the side and will bill you $80 for the whole thing or $30/h and so on. If you are a master at something, ensure you get valued for that or you will get treated as a jack of all trades and master of none. Nothing wrong with the latter, but society looks down on it, and people respect more the specialist! I believe this stems from the fact that small businesses and more people plunge into the

ACKNOWLEDGMENT!

"I do it all" kind of service to try to get more calls and make more money. This attitude kind of washes out this type of worker, and they see you as a fly-by-night operation versus the expert who has spent years and years mastering one field – that gets admired and respected more.

MARCELLO

CHAPTER 5
THE DONTGIVEASHIT

You are talking to your client at a meeting, and you can spot right away if she/he is listening. Are they making eye contact while you speak? Is their head slightly canted? Is she/he doing anything else while you talk? These are the crucial signs that will tell you if they are listening.

The worst sign of all is when they get on their phone, and they pretend to be doing something or if you are at a coffee shop or at a restaurant, they will pour themselves water or wine, start eating bread, move their chair, fold the napkin, look elsewhere, etc.

I get it, in a diner or a restaurant, during a business meeting, the point is to talk and eat, but their timing while doing so will reveal their listening level.

This one time, this client which I met at a Starbucks, kept getting calls; that's rude, man! In a meeting, you shut that thing down, and you let it go to a voicemail or get yourself an assistant motherfuc… He just kept doing something every time I was going to start a point or to let him know of something important (costs, details of the service, etc.).

This is psychology, some of them are aware of doing that, they don't listen or pretend not to listen on purpose by looking elsewhere or making themselves a bit busy as to not give you attention or shall I say **acknowledgment**?

When you are talking to someone, and you are telling them something important (it is no small chat), if the other person does not look into your eyes and/or looks distracted, it is like saying: I do not really care about what you are saying, you do not count. Your voice starts confident, but when seeing this type of attitude or moreover, this subtle ignoring behavior, you could lose conviction.

It is almost like the other person, the customer, purposefully wants to start hearing the cracks in your voice. Is it a test? Do they want to see how confident you are? Or how much you believe in what you have to offer? Possible.

What I do in this case, is I call them by their first name and a bit louder as to pull them back to you, maybe ask them a question to re-grab their attention and then redirect to your sale-spiel or whatever you are saying.

Another strategy: you could continue talking while you are purposefully being ignored, and you can now start doing the same. For example, suddenly, you could pull your phone out while you talk or make yourself distracted like they do, and ironically, when doing that, they start looking at you again. It is now them feeling like they are not given the attention. That is when you kick back in your attention towards them and re-establish a connection, bzzzz...bzzzz...hissss...ROGER.

I let it not bother me, and I continue as if I had their full attention because, in the end, I thought to myself: I am not worried, he is going to have to read and sign the contract anyway which is repeating exactly what I am telling him now, even better. To the reader: for your information, my contracts are separated into two parts. The first is made of readable words that actually give you simple and precise information in big font, and I require initials on the most pungent sections (pricing, cancellations, refunds, etc.), the stuff you want to know; the second part is made of the legal mumbo jumbo that only lawyers understand. I care that they truly read and understand what an agreement says, what my services involve, and that they know the cons, if any, in advance.

However, this is the dontgiveashit customer, and as such, do not expect from him/her to even open the email to read and sign the damn agreement. In that particular case, he did not, and after one week of chasing him via email and several, gradual texts, he replies saying something along the lines: Oh yeah, I did not have time and the blah blah blah. I messaged him back and said: you ignored our agreement, all my texts and emails, and your only super late reply did not show any care. I mailed back your check; I will no longer offer my services to you. Thank you and stay well!

Was he a professional? Certainly not. Does this customer fit the acknowledgment test? Not by miles. Here is what could happen if you continue dealing with this customer because you fear losing the money, the sale, etc.: he will drag you down for months and never reach the deadline you had initially set with him. He will not be punctual paying you, most likely, he will pay you real late after you rendered your services. He will think he can control you, slap you, and you will be his slave. Once you settle, in for a penny, in for a pound, yeah?

CHAPTER 6
OTHER STORIES

I could go on and on and tell you thousands of stories that happened to me with different clients, but I believe it wouldn't help further the point of this guide. I could tell you about the husband that hired me to fix his computer, and later, when I returned it to his house, he pretended to have never seen me in front of his wife, that he never even spoke to me or hired me. LOL.

I felt I was being punked there. It was surreal. Besides the fact I had a recording of the phone conversation with him plus his signature on the repair contract with all of his information. When I showed it to the wife, she just pulled her credit card to pay in shame, and I was gone from that mental place. *What the writer of this book did not know is that he had just entered the Twilight Zone.*

Or the gentleman that bought a laptop from me, and asked me to teach him all about how to use a computer, from opening an email, sending messages, using various software, how to customize his background, colors, how to scan for viruses, how to print, scan, and God knows how many questions he had for me, for like 7 straight hours!

MARCELLO

The next day he asks for his money back in an email, out of the blue and for no reason. Cold like a shark!

We had quite an exchange of messages, and in the end, he apologized and explained to me he was not feeling well, and the day after my tutoring and after buying the laptop, he had a heart attack. Sometimes, you are not dealing with an asshole customer, and an unexpected reason might lurk behind it. It is important that you dig deeper to try to understand the real reasons behind such an absurd and nonsense attitude.

The lady that called me after buying a computer from me, and with no appointment and out of the blue went on asking me about why this word file wasn't working anymore. I was like: not sure, but I can diagnose it for you if we schedule an appointment. She wanted to sue me instead because I sold her a computer where this document file would not open; this was 3 years after selling her the computer. It is not like I created that file on her behalf anyway, or how on Earth could I possibly be responsible for her files or the functionality of the Word software? I said: I only sold you a computer lady and that was ages ago. I am not responsible for your files, you are insane, and yes, I will see you in court.

I can only imagine Judge Judy frying this lady on TV, not that she would have taken her mental case anyway.

CHAPTER 7
CONCLUSION

I would like to say I only mentioned towards the end what I do for a living because I did not want you to create any conjectures about my type of work. Who knows, maybe you thought of a computer expert and website designer pricing to be only $10 per hour. I wanted you to follow my stories clearly and not be fogged in any way by what I do. It does not matter what you do, what you sell, what company you run, as long as you are and/or wish to be your own boss, you will have to command respect from your customers and respect them the same way.

The point of this guide, hopefully, is to have inspired you a bit. Maybe you got something out of it; you can use it to spot a good customer or the asshole that is not going to bring any profit or joy to your business.

Maybe you will be able to know in advance who you are dealing with, and this could save you thousands of headaches, ridiculous / possible lawsuits, unnecessary refunds, loss of work / time/labor, and tons of negativity.

You will avoid the toxic client and deal only with professionals or people with common sense, a certain level of respect for others and good manners.

More importantly, you will know to focus on getting **acknowledgment,** which dresses you with dignity, respect and positivity. Like a magnet, attract only the good, the compatible, the right client.

You will start enjoying running your business daily; you will be your own boss because you are in charge of your own business. And why not? You can apply this method to your life as well.

www.ingramcontent.com/pod-product-compliance
Lightning Source LLC
Chambersburg PA
CBHW050322220526
45465CB00005B/2097